Natural Writer

Natural Writer

**A Story about
Marjorie Kinnan Rawlings**

by Judy Cook and Laura Lee Smith
illustrated by Laurie Harden

A Creative Minds Biography

Carolrhoda Books, Inc./Minneapolis

To Josephine Agnes Readie, with love

Text copyright © 2001 by Judy Cook and Laura Lee Smith
Illustrations copyright © 2001 by Laurie Harden

Carolrhoda Books, Inc.
A division of Lerner Publishing Group
241 First Avenue North
Minneapolis, MN 55401 U.S.A.

Website address: www.lernerbooks.com

Library of Congress Cataloging-in-Publication Data

Cook, Judy, 1943–
   Natural writer: a story about Marjorie Kinnan Rawlings / by Judy Cook
and Laura Lee Smith ; illustrated by Laurie Harden.
      p.   cm. — (A creative minds biography)
   Includes bibliographical references and index.
   ISBN 1-57505-468-X (lib. bdg. : alk. paper)
      1. Rawlings, Marjorie Kinnan, 1896–1953—Juvenile literature.
2. Authors, American—20th century—Biography—Juvenile literature.
3. Women pioneers—Florida—Biography—Juvenile literature. 4. Frontier
and pioneer life—Florida—Juvenile literature. [1. Rawlings, Marjorie
Kinnan, 1896–1953. 2. Authors, American. 3. Women—Biography.]
I. Smith, Laura Lee, 1968– II. Harden, Laurie, ill. III. Title. IV. Series.
PS3535.A845 Z63 2001
813'.52—dc21   00-009657

Manufactured in the United States of America
1 2 3 4 5 6 - MA - 06 05 04 03 02 01

Table of Contents

1

Storyteller

"Hurry, hurry," a young boy yelled as he ran down the cobblestone street at twilight. "Marjorie's going to tell stories!" Hot, sweaty children quickly left their games of hide-and-seek and ran to the nearby church. They huddled together on the church's cool steps. It was the first day of summer vacation, and many children were allowed to stay out after dark. In just a few minutes, the lamplighter would light the gas street-lamps, and the storytelling session would begin.

Marjorie Kinnan smiled to herself. Then she stood and proudly walked to the front of the group of children gathered on the steps.

Marjorie was a pretty girl, with long brown hair, fair skin, and large gray-blue eyes. She had a round face and small hands and feet. Someone who didn't know her might have thought that she was shy and ladylike. But Marjorie was a tomboy at heart, and she loved being in front of an audience. She knew that all eyes were watching her closely, and her mind spun with the story she was about to tell. Scary stories were the most popular kind of story among the children in her neighborhood. Marjorie had a special treat in store tonight.

After the older children had gotten the younger ones to settle down, Marjorie took a deep breath and began a tale about a wild wolf. As her story grew more intense, squeals and giggles went up from the audience. The trembling children held their breath. Suddenly, Marjorie threw her head back, opened her mouth wide, and howled.

One of the littlest boys in the audience covered his ears and screamed. Marjorie was forced to stop until the other children quieted him down. She scowled at him, knowing the pace of her story had been interrupted. That boy was too young to listen to her wolf stories, she thought. "You'll have to take Jimmy home now," she declared when she finished the first story. "There's going to be a wolf in the next one."

Marjorie Kinnan was born August 8, 1896, into a wealthy family. Her father, Arthur Kinnan, was a lawyer who worked at the United States Patent Office. Arthur was very successful and could afford to give his family many luxuries. The family owned two pieces of property. During the school year, the Kinnans lived in a quiet suburb of Washington, D.C. They spent the summer months on their dairy farm in Maryland.

Marjorie's mother, Ida Traphagen Kinnan, preferred the house in town, with its lace curtains and Victorian furniture. Ida was less fond of farm life. She liked having her embroidery club come for afternoon tea much more than she liked cooking over campfires and spending time outdoors. But Marjorie and her younger brother, Arthur Jr., loved being on the farm. They slept in tents and spent long hours playing in the open fields and exploring the little brook that ran along the pasture. Marjorie spied on rabbits as they scurried across the fields. She recognized different kinds of birds as they flew through the trees. And she loved to dig in the garden and watch it grow.

On weekends, Marjorie and her father often passed their time studying the trees and plants on the farm. They talked about birds and butterflies, scanned the trees for owls, and listened to the chatter of crickets.

Arthur Kinnan shared his love of the land with his daughter and patiently answered all of Marjorie's questions. They even had a secret signal between them—a birdcall that they perfected over the summer months. When Arthur returned to the farm after a day of work in the city, he would whistle the birdcall. Then Marjorie would come running down the hill to meet him.

It seemed as though Marjorie lived two lives. On the farm during the hot summers, she was a free spirit. But back in school in Washington, D.C., Marjorie resigned herself to the ladylike behavior her mother expected. Although she didn't like to, Marjorie wore the starchy white dresses and frilly collars that Ida picked out for her. She helped with the housework, studied hard, and earned good grades, especially in English.

Marjorie was a good student, but she was an even better storyteller. When she wasn't keeping the neighborhood children on the edge of their seats with her stories, she also liked to write. Her first poem, about a pair of bluebirds, was called "Mr. and Mrs. Bluebird." Marjorie found that putting her stories and poems on paper gave life to the wonderful characters in her imagination.

When Marjorie was eleven, she decided to enter one of her stories in a contest sponsored by the

Washington Post, a large newspaper. She won a two-dollar prize, and the paper printed her story on the Sunday children's page. Seeing her words in print was thrilling! A dream began to take shape in Marjorie's mind. Someday, she believed, she would become a famous writer.

Marjorie's family was excited for her. Ida encouraged Marjorie. She was even willing to release Marjorie from household chores so that she could work on her stories. "If you have an inspiration," her mother told her, "you may go and write." Clever Marjorie soon became "inspired" whenever it was her turn to dust the furniture.

During high school, Marjorie continued to write and to send her stories to contests and magazines. She entered one of her short stories, called "The Reincarnation of Miss Hetty," in a contest sponsored by *McCall's* magazine. She won seventy-five dollars for her story —a great deal of money in 1912.

Marjorie knew that her dreams made her unusual. Most young women did not plan for careers. Many of Marjorie's girlfriends wanted to get married and start a family. They weren't interested in working outside the home. But Marjorie was different. She didn't want the kind of life her mother lived. She wasn't interested in having luncheons and tea parties for her lady friends. Marjorie wanted a life of adventure and excitement. And she wanted to write wonderful stories that would make people laugh and cry. She knew in her heart that writing would make her happy.

2

Songs of a Housewife

Marjorie was still in high school when tragedy struck the Kinnan family. Her father learned he had a deadly kidney disease. Marjorie was heartbroken as she watched him grow weaker and weaker. He died in the winter of 1913, when Marjorie was sixteen years old. To Marjorie, it felt as though a "great and terrible stillness" covered the earth the day her father died.

After Arthur Kinnan's death, and after Marjorie graduated from high school, Ida decided to move the family to Madison, Wisconsin. They had friends in Madison, and Arthur had wanted Marjorie to go to the University of Wisconsin.

In the fall of 1914, Marjorie enrolled at the university as an English major. Although she missed her father terribly, she forced herself to focus on her studies. She became an honor student, and she received many awards for her achievements in school. She was also popular, and she kept very busy with new friends and school activities.

Marjorie still loved being in front of an audience. She often acted in plays with a women's drama club called the Red Dominos. And, of course, she wrote. Marjorie had already decided that the way to be a successful writer was through hard work and determination. She wasn't afraid of the challenge. She took classes in literature and creative writing, where she read poems and stories by British authors. She studied hard, often long into the night. Her professors saw her talent and encouraged her.

Along with her classes, Marjorie gained experience writing for the college yearbook and newspaper. At the newspaper, she met a tall, handsome young man who was also a writer. They spent many hours working together. Before long, Marjorie began to see Charles, or Chuck, Rawlings as more than a friend.

She decided he was the man she wanted to marry, and it was clear that Chuck felt the same way about her. The two made up their minds to follow their writing dreams as a couple.

Marjorie and Chuck wanted to marry right after graduation, but World War I stood in their way. The United States had recently gotten involved in the war. Chuck wanted to "join the colors," or serve his country by fighting the battles raging in Europe. Many of their friends had already left college to fight overseas. Marjorie knew that some of them had died in the war, and she worried about Chuck. But Chuck could be as stubborn as Marjorie.

When Chuck and Marjorie graduated in 1918, they became engaged. Then Chuck enlisted in the army. He was sent to a training camp in New York. Marjorie decided to move to New York City to be near him. She would try to earn a living as a writer. After her success at college, she believed more than ever that she had the talent to write. And her work on the college newspaper and yearbook gave her job experience. Marjorie was confident that she would find a job as a writer and sell her stories to magazines.

Ida Kinnan was worried. Marjorie alone in a city the size of New York? It was an unusual life for a young woman, and it seemed too dangerous to

Marjorie's mother. She was concerned for Marjorie's safety and well-being. She was also concerned about the engagement to Chuck. He seemed like a nice young man, but Ida had doubts. The relationship between the two young people was unpredictable. They were both headstrong and stubborn people. Ida thought Chuck was not the right man for Marjorie. "If you could explain to me just what you love about him," she told Marjorie, "perhaps I could understand the interest a little better." Ida's remarks about Chuck and New York only made Marjorie angry.

Ida could see it was hopeless to argue. Once Marjorie made her mind up to do something, there was very little that could stop her. So Ida packed her bags and went with Marjorie to New York. She had to convince herself that Marjorie would be all right and that she had a decent place to live. Marjorie rented a room in a boardinghouse and settled into what she hoped would be a successful, exciting life. She promised her mother that she would be fine. Ida finally left her daughter and returned to Wisconsin. "Mother is really satisfied I can take care of myself," Marjorie wrote in a letter to Chuck.

But things didn't go well for Marjorie. Her stories were continually turned down by magazines. Editors needed interesting stories that would help sell more magazines. But Marjorie was still writing stories in the style that she learned in college. She tried to write like the British writers she had studied. And she wrote about characters and towns that did not exist in American life. Her stories did not ring true to American magazine editors.

Marjorie was becoming discouraged. She was alone, and she missed Chuck terribly. No one wanted to buy her stories, and she was struggling to find work. Without the praise and encouragement from her college professors, Marjorie started to doubt herself. She began to wonder if she would ever succeed as a writer.

The one bright spot in her life was her upcoming marriage. The couple wrote each other long letters. In her letters, Marjorie told Chuck how much she missed him. She also poured out her dreams of success, excitement, and adventure. She was anxious to get married, but she couldn't stand the idea of being settled like so many of her friends. She wanted excitement—to see the world and to write about it. "Why not do something fascinating while we're young and peppy?" she asked Chuck. "If we don't do it now, we never will."

In 1918 the war in Europe ended, and Chuck left the army before he had a chance to go overseas.

Marjorie married him in May 1919. Although the couple talked of great adventures, Chuck was not as adventurous as Marjorie. He was also under pressure from his family to return to his hometown of Rochester, New York. The Rawlings family hoped that Chuck would join his father's shoe business. But Marjorie did not want to live in Rochester. She convinced Chuck to accept an advertising job at a company in New York City instead. When the company went out of business months later, the disappointed couple had to change their plans.

Luckily, friends told Marjorie and Chuck about some newspaper jobs in Louisville, Kentucky. They jumped at the opportunity to make a living as writers. Marjorie was pleased to be writing for pay at last, but she and Chuck weren't paid enough to survive. After two years in Louisville, Chuck accepted a job with his father. He felt that it was the only way he could earn a decent living. Much to Marjorie's dismay, the couple moved to Rochester. Chuck began working as a traveling shoe salesman, and for a time, Marjorie lived a very settled life.

As usual, Marjorie made the best of a difficult situation. If she had to live in Rochester, then at least she would find interesting work. By the fall of 1922, she had found jobs writing for several local newspapers.

Marjorie wrote articles for the Rochester *Evening Journal* and the Rochester *America*. In 1926 she began writing a daily column called "Songs of the Housewife" for the *Times-Union*. For the column, she wrote poems with titles like "Last Night's Dishes," "Making the Beds," and "The Housewife's Heaven." Although Marjorie wrote a daily column about being a housewife, a housewife was the last thing she wanted to be.

The newspaper jobs weren't perfect, but they taught her new skills. Her typing ability improved, and she learned to write in a way that appealed to readers. Her work also taught her how to interview people and how to make interesting stories out of real-life people and events.

As time went on, however, Marjorie became discouraged about her life. She knew that she didn't want to be a journalist forever. But her dreams of being a famous writer seemed far away. The stories she sent out to magazines were rejected again and again. No one wanted to publish them. Her marriage had also become a problem. Marjorie disliked the fact that Chuck traveled in his job and was away for long periods of time. Chuck was jealous of some of the friendships Marjorie made at the newspaper— especially her friendships with other men. The couple argued often. As time went on, Marjorie became more and more unhappy. She longed for some real excitement and adventure. She found both on a trip to Florida.

3

Making the Move

Marjorie and Chuck thought that a vacation and a change of scenery might help ease some of the tension in their marriage. In March 1928, they decided to visit Chuck's two brothers. Jimmy and Wray Rawlings were living in central Florida. Marjorie and Chuck sailed on a steamship from New York to Jacksonville, Florida. When they arrived at the dock, they were met by an energetic woman named Zelma Cason. Zelma was matter-of-fact, down-to-earth, and casual. She was different from the refined, cultured women Marjorie knew in the north. Zelma took the Rawlingses by car from

Jacksonville into the barely populated land of central Florida. There they met up with Chuck's brothers in a small town called Island Grove.

Marjorie was amazed by the sights of Florida. It seemed like such a wild, unsettled land. She smelled sweet orange blossoms and felt hot wind on her face. She saw thick, lush vegetation surrounding the few houses and barns they came across. And she saw dozens of animals wandering freely in the wilderness: deer, raccoons, armadillos, turtles, snakes—even alligators. Something stirred inside Marjorie. This place was beautiful and peaceful. It reminded her of summers she spent on the farm in Maryland when she was a child. She felt that she had finally arrived home.

Marjorie and Chuck had a wonderful vacation. They hunted and fished and relaxed. Before long, Marjorie was pleading with Chuck to agree to move south. "Oh, how we could write!" she exclaimed. She was convinced that the quiet Florida wilderness would inspire them. Chuck agreed. Soon after they returned to Rochester, they decided to buy property in Florida and move there in the fall. They sold their furnishings, packed their belongings, and bid good-bye to their family and friends.

For thirty-two-year-old Marjorie, the move was the exciting adventure that she had been waiting for since college.   Florida was far away from her family, friends, and daily routine.   She would escape the long hours and late-night assignments of her newspaper job.   And she would leave city life behind.   She believed that her creative spirit would finally be free.

The Rawlingses had asked Chuck's brothers to arrange for the purchase of a seventy-four-acre farm and orange grove in the small town of Cross Creek, Florida. The couple saw it for the first time on the day that they moved in.   Marjorie arrived at the farm excited and impatient to begin her new life. But her heart sank a little at the sight of the shabby farmhouse that was to be her new home. It was run-down and badly in need of paint. The roof and porch seemed sloped and unsteady, and the rooms were all painted a dingy gray.   There wasn't even a bathroom. But Marjorie was determined to make it work. With the help of Wray and Jimmy, she and Chuck got to work fixing up the farmhouse and taking over the operations of the orange grove.

Marjorie and Chuck hoped to earn a living selling oranges from the orange grove. That way they could spend long hours writing. They did not realize just how much work the grove needed.   Marjorie had thought she was prepared for farm life. But she was wrong. Life on her farm in Florida was very different from life on her childhood farm in Maryland.

At Cross Creek, fences had to be mended, cows needed to be milked, and the orange grove and garden needed care. Even daily chores were difficult. Marjorie cooked big meals on a wood-burning stove and washed dirty clothes in an iron pot. While working, she might catch a terrible case of poison ivy or stumble into a patch of thorny sandspurs. She had to learn to live with mosquitoes, chiggers, ants, and snakes. And the heat! Sometimes it seemed completely unbearable.

It was a hard life, but Marjorie refused to give up. She found ways to make the best of bad days on the farm. Once, she let out her frustration by screaming. She screamed and screamed until she felt better. A while later, two of her neighbors came up to the gate to check on her. Marjorie realized then that her screaming had been heard for some distance. Embarrassed, she assured them she was all right, saying, "Perhaps you heard me—singing." After that, Marjorie often laughingly told people that she lived within screaming distance of her neighbors.

Despite the hardships and the annoyances of living on the farm, Marjorie truly loved being there. She loved to walk from the sunshine into the cool shade of the orange grove. She loved watching the redbirds build their nests in the magnolia trees and the quail scurry across the yard. And she loved sitting on her porch at night, quiet except for the sound of crickets and frogs. She began to think of her farm, and all of Cross Creek, as an "enchanted land."

Several months after she moved to Cross Creek, Marjorie got the chance to explore more of the Florida wilderness. Her friend Zelma Cason had been hired by the local government to take a census. It was Zelma's job to take a count of all the people living in the scrub—the countryside surrounding Cross Creek. Zelma thought Marjorie would enjoy the trip, so she invited her new neighbor to join her. The two women set off on horseback because many of the homes were off the main road and could not be reached by car.

During the trip, Marjorie met some of the people who lived in the most isolated areas around Cross Creek. These people lived off the land. They survived by hunting, fishing, and growing their own vegetables. They raised their families in simple wooden houses with tin roofs, and they made do with what little they had. By big city standards, they were poor. But it seemed to Marjorie that they were content and at peace with their surroundings.

The people who lived in the Florida scrub were often called "Crackers." The nickname may have come from early settlers in Florida, who cracked their whips as they rode in their wagons. Or it may have come from the way the Florida natives cracked dry corn to make cornmeal. Either way, it was a name that stuck.

Back at Cross Creek, Marjorie made an effort to get to know her neighbors. She enjoyed talking to them and listening to the way they spoke. Marjorie's Cracker neighbors had a gentleness about them, and they used words that were different from words Marjorie used. They spoke of critters and varmints, antses and skeeters, lizards and gators. Marjorie tried hard to fit in with her neighbors and to respect their way of life. She was friendly, and her new friends found her easy to talk to. Marjorie happily gave up her city clothes and began to wear casual, loose-fitting housedresses like the other women at the Creek. Sometimes she even wore jeans and boots like the men.

Some people thought the Crackers were ignorant and crude, but Marjorie accepted them just the way they were. She was never critical of the rough ways of the people at Cross Creek. It didn't take long before the Creek neighbors began to accept Marjorie. She wanted to learn everything about the Cracker lifestyle. And her neighbors were more than willing to teach her.

Marjorie was feeling more and more at home in Florida, and she was learning to take the challenges of farm life in stride. Chuck was another story. The hardships of life at the Creek were becoming too much for him. He longed for the city life he and Marjorie once had. He began to write for several newspapers, and he traveled to research stories.

In a way, Marjorie didn't blame him. She often thought to herself that a person would have to be a little bit crazy to live at the Creek. But the idea suited her just fine. She liked her unusual life. She loved the isolation, the hard work, the simplicity, and the peace. Best of all, she was finding time to write.

Marjorie worked hard. She got up very early every day to do all her chores for the farm. When she finished, she worked on her stories. She spent hours at her typewriter, which she had set up on her screened porch to protect her from the mosquitoes. For a while, the same frustrating pattern she had run into up north continued. She sent her stories out to magazines, but they were rejected again and again. Marjorie knew she needed to write about something new and different. But what? The answer came from an unexpected source—her neighbors.

It was as if the answer had been staring her in the face the whole time. She just hadn't seen it. Stories about Florida Crackers—this was the new idea she had been searching for. Life in and around the Creek was an unusual subject that she believed would interest magazine readers. The people she met at the Creek were completely different from anyone she had met before. Changes in the rest of the country had not yet caught up with them. Living in the backwoods kept them isolated. The only things in their lives were the necessities—food, clothing, shelter. But although they lacked luxuries, they did not lack dignity. They were friendly and neighborly to everyone, even a northern "Yankee" like Marjorie. She couldn't think of another topic she would rather write about.

Marjorie put her training as a journalist to work. She carefully recorded the world around her. She interviewed her neighbors and wrote down the stories they told her about their lives at Cross Creek. She also learned the names of the trees, shrubs, flowers, birds, and other creatures that lived in the wilderness surrounding her new home. She filled notebooks with descriptions of the people, wildlife, and vegetation. Then she used the information to create believable characters and stories.

Marjorie sent some of the stories she had written about Cross Creek to *Scribner's Magazine* in New York City. She called the stories "Cracker Chidlings."

As she waited for a response from the magazine, she wondered if her stories would be rejected once again. Maybe they were not as special as she thought. But soon enough, Marjorie received the good news she had been hoping for. *Scribner's* decided to accept "Cracker Chidlings" for publication! After so many years of rejection, Marjorie was thrilled to see her work published in such a major literary magazine. Marjorie was thirty-four years old when "Cracker Chidlings" came out in February 1931.

Encouraged by the success of "Cracker Chidlings," Marjorie submitted another story to *Scribner's*. "Jacob's Ladder" was about a young Cracker couple struggling to live off the land in the Big Scrub, the wilderness area not far from Cross Creek. This story, too, was published in 1931. When a check for seven hundred dollars arrived as payment, Marjorie immediately decided to spend it on an indoor bathroom for the farmhouse.

Finally, finally, after years of struggle, Marjorie was beginning to publish writing she could be proud of. She had done what she had longed to do all her life. And she hoped this would be only the beginning.

4

Life at the Creek

Marjorie realized she was on to something with her writing. Her tales of the Florida Crackers and their simple ways of living seemed to appeal to readers. Her writing had even caught the attention of Max Perkins, the chief editor at Scribner's, which published books and *Scribner's Magazine.* Max was a very important man in the publishing business. He was an editor to some of the greatest writers of American literature, including Ernest Hemingway, Thomas Wolfe, and F. Scott Fitzgerald.

Max was a quiet, intelligent man with a special gift for helping writers express themselves. Marjorie's stories about life in Florida had left an impression on him, and he was interested in publishing more of her work. Through letters, he began to give Marjorie the praise and encouragement that she needed to do her best. He became one of her most valued friends.

Max liked Marjorie's stories so much that he thought she should write a novel about life in the wild Florida scrub. She immediately began to follow his advice. She worked closely with Max on the book, and she soon began to depend on his guidance.

Marjorie wanted to make her characters and the Florida scrub come to life in her novel. To do that, she felt that she needed to spend time with a Cracker family. In the late summer of 1931, Marjorie decided to spend more than two months living with an old woman named Piety Fiddia and her son, Leonard. The Fiddias were true Florida Crackers. Marjorie and Leonard hunted squirrel and deer, made their own whiskey, and fished for mullet. Marjorie worked side by side with Piety, making homemade soap and scrubbing the floors of the rough cabin. She also listened to their stories and asked them many questions. From the Fiddias, Marjorie learned what life for Florida Crackers was truly like. Then she took what she had learned and shaped it into her first novel, *South Moon Under.*

When *South Moon Under* was published in March 1933, it was well received. Marjorie was thrilled to learn that people enjoyed reading about life in rural Florida. Unfortunately, Chuck couldn't seem to share Marjorie's happiness over the success of her work. Instead he took every opportunity to criticize her. His own writing career was not doing as well as he would have liked, and Marjorie felt that he took his frustrations out on her. She began to grow tired of his anger and unhappiness. She thought having more money would make things easier, but it only seemed to upset Chuck even more. He could not forget that the money was coming from Marjorie's successes, not his.

Marjorie was disheartened. She still cared for Chuck, but she could see that he was not happy at the Creek. And he was making her life miserable. Chuck left Marjorie and Cross Creek in March 1933, and Marjorie filed for divorce.

To forget her loneliness, Marjorie decided to join her friend Dessie Vinson Smith on a boat trip down Florida's St. Johns River. She hoped the adventure would give her more ideas for stories. Marjorie and her friend planned to cover several hundred miles and take many days to complete their journey. Marjorie knew it would be an excellent opportunity to learn more about the land and the people who had become so important to her writing and so close to her heart.

Friends warned the women of the dangers they might face alone on their trip. But Marjorie and Dessie could not be stopped. They set off in an eighteen-foot rowboat with a small outboard motor. Dessie was an avid sportswoman who knew how to take care of herself in the backwoods. Marjorie willingly placed herself in Dessie's capable hands. The two women loaded up their little boat with food, camping gear, and guns. Then they set off down the St. Johns River. They floated through acres of water hyacinths and watched alligators basking on the shore. They saw white egrets hunting for food and occasionally passed a lone fisher enjoying the solitude. The trip did indeed provide Marjorie with new material, and she returned to Cross Creek bursting with new stories, eager to start writing again.

By November 1933, the divorce between Marjorie and Chuck was final. They were both hurt and angry with each other. The failure of the marriage was a bitter disappointment for Marjorie, but in some ways she was relieved that it was all over. "Life just wasn't worth living with the black cloud of his daily disagreeableness over me," she wrote to a friend.

39

As time went on, Marjorie gradually began to feel a sense of peace and calm. "The sun shines again," she said, "and when I wake up in the morning I feel like a normal human being, instead of being filled with dread waiting for the first ugly remark." The divorce marked the beginning of a new kind of independence. Marjorie could focus on her writing and her life at the Creek without feeling guilty about Chuck. But life wouldn't be easy without him.

The country was in the midst of the Great Depression. During this time, jobs were scarce, and many Americans struggled with poverty. Marjorie was earning a small living from her writing and the orange grove, but it often wasn't enough. She needed money to pay old debts and to make repairs to the farmhouse. Sometimes Marjorie had no money in the bank. It got so bad that one day in the fall of 1933, the only food in her house was a box of crackers and a can of tomato soup. Things seemed bleak until the mailman arrived. He delivered a letter informing Marjorie that one of her short stories, "Gal Young Un," had won the famous O. Henry Award. Along with the letter was a check for five hundred dollars. Life at the Creek could continue.

Marjorie knew that if she wanted to make a living as a writer, she needed help with all the work of the orange grove. She wanted to build on her success as an author. And her mind was brimming with stories. But the demands of running the farm were taking up nearly all of her time. Somehow she found the money to hire a manager for the farm and a woman to help with the work in the house. With hired help running the farm and the house, Marjorie was finally able to spend long hours at her typewriter on the porch. She was ready to get on with her writing.

5

The Yearling

In 1934 Marjorie was hard at work on her second novel, *Golden Apples.* But she was also thinking a lot about another idea that Max had suggested to her. "I am thinking of a book about a boy," he had told her. "A book about a boy and the life of the scrub is the thing we want." He thought that a book about life in the Florida wilderness would be perfect for young readers who liked adventure.

At first Marjorie resisted, but the idea brought back memories of her storytelling sessions in Washington, D.C. She had loved those nightly sessions on the church steps. She remembered the thrill of weaving her tales and scaring the boys. After mulling it over for some time, she suggested to Max an idea for a story. "I think it cannot help but be very beautiful," she wrote.

Marjorie got her idea from a friend named Cal Long. Cal's family had been one of the first to move to the scrub country in the 1870s. Marjorie remembered a story he had told her about a deer that he kept as a pet when he was a boy. Cal never forgot the day that his father told him to kill the fawn because it would not stop eating the family's food supply. Cal and his father knew the fawn was a wild animal and could never be tamed. Marjorie wanted to write a novel about a hardworking Cracker family and a young boy who tried to keep a fawn as a pet. She knew it would make a dramatic story that would appeal to both young and adult readers.

Max agreed that her idea was a good one. But she still had many other things taking up her time. She was struggling to complete *Golden Apples*. She was also traveling a great deal. In addition, there were the constant demands of the farm and the grove to deal with. But through it all, the idea of a young boy and his pet fawn kept coming back to her. Slowly but surely, the book began to take shape. And Max encouraged Marjorie through his letters every step of the way.

In September 1936, Marjorie moved into a rented cabin in the mountains of North Carolina. She knew that she needed to get away from the demands and distractions of the farm. That would allow her to write her new book. In the cool, clear air of the mountains, a story began to unfold.

In her new novel, Marjorie described the life of a twelve-year-old boy named Jody Baxter. Jody and his parents live in the scrub. They deal with many hardships as they try to survive in the Florida wilderness. Marjorie remembered her own family as she wrote about Jody and his family. Jody and his father, Penny Baxter, share a bond like Marjorie and her own father did. The two Baxters even signal each other with a special birdcall.

Jody helps raise a fawn into a yearling—a one-year-old deer. He names his pet deer Flag. Marjorie used her imagination to describe Jody's relationship with Flag. She also imagined how difficult it would be for Jody to choose between his fawn and protecting his family's way of life.

Marjorie hoped to share with her readers the true struggle that families living in the scrub faced. She was not afraid to write about the hardships and tragedies of life. But she also wanted to describe the joy and peace young Jody finds in his stark existence.

45

She wanted her readers to experience the wonder of nature through Jody's eyes. And she wanted readers to understand the way Jody could love a fawn like Flag. She carefully described how Jody feels when he befriends Flag:

> The fawn lifted its nose, scenting him. [Jody] reached out one hand and laid it on the soft neck. The touch made him delirious. He moved forward on all fours until he was close beside it. He put his arms around its body.... He stroked its sides as gently as though the fawn were a china deer and he might break it. Its skin was softer than the white 'coonskin knapsack. It was sleek and clean and had a sweet scent of grass. He rose slowly and lifted the fawn from the ground.

As she neared the end of her work on the novel, Marjorie struggled with ideas for a title. She finally settled on *The Yearling*. Her "boy's book" came out in February of 1938, when Marjorie was forty-one.

The Yearling was a huge success. Within months Marjorie became a celebrity, and she soon found herself attending parties where she met other famous writers. The book became a national best-seller. MGM Studios even bought the movie rights to the story. They wanted to make the novel into a film.

In 1939 Marjorie received more good news. *The Yearling* had been awarded the Pulitzer Prize for fiction! This was one of the most famous writing awards in the world. Marjorie could hardly believe her good fortune. "I really thought I'd had as much luck as I deserved on one book," she wrote to a friend.

Marjorie had been dreaming of becoming a famous writer since she'd been a child. *The Yearling* made this dream come true. But more important, Marjorie knew without a doubt that her book touched the lives of many, many readers. Thousands of people wrote to her telling her how the story had affected their lives. She was deeply moved by the letters. They meant more to her than money or fame. To Marjorie, they were a true mark of success.

The success of *The Yearling* also meant that Marjorie was earning more money than ever before. A year after *The Yearling* was published, Marjorie bought a cottage on the ocean near St. Augustine, Florida. St. Augustine was a small town a couple hours away from Cross Creek. The cottage was a place where she could go to escape the heat and demands of the farm. Here she could also recover from an illness that had become a serious health problem. Marjorie was suffering from diverticulosis, a painful inflammation of the intestines.

For the first time in many years, she began to spend time away from her beloved Cross Creek. It was a quiet place for her to work on her writing. But there was another reason Marjorie was spending time in St. Augustine, and his name was Norton Baskin.

6

Trouble in Cross Creek

Marjorie had met Norton Baskin shortly after her divorce from Chuck. He was a handsome, charming man who made a living as a hotel manager. Like Marjorie, he was quick to laugh, and he loved to have a good time. Norton was also kind, generous, and accepting. The two enjoyed being together, and they cared deeply for each other. Marjorie was in no rush to give up her independence. Still, she had been thinking more and more about making a new life with Norton. They decided to marry in October 1941, eight years after Marjorie's divorce from Chuck. After their wedding, Norton and Marjorie moved into the top floor of Norton's Castle Warden hotel in St. Augustine.

Marjorie had been spending a lot of time with Norton, but she hadn't stopped writing. With Max's encouragement, she had been working on another book. This one was about her own life at Cross Creek. In the book, she wrote about her friends and neighbors, using their actual names. Marjorie made the book as realistic as possible. She wanted each detail to bring the world of Cross Creek to life. "I have used true names in practically every instance," she told Max. But she was also careful to protect the privacy of the people at Cross Creek. "I have tried not to put things so that anyone's feelings would be hurt. These people are my friends and neighbors, and I would not be unkind for anything." When *Cross Creek* came out in February of 1942, the book became another best-seller for Marjorie.

Marjorie had asked most of her friends for permission to write about them. But she had neglected to ask one person, Zelma Cason. She had known Zelma longer than almost anyone at Cross Creek. It was Zelma who had first welcomed Marjorie to Florida at the dock in Jacksonville many years earlier. Marjorie assumed that since Zelma was such a good friend, she wouldn't mind if Marjorie mentioned her in the book. But Zelma did mind. She was furious when she read Marjorie's description of her in *Cross Creek*.

To Marjorie, the description was accurate and honest. It brought out Zelma as a real person. But to

Zelma, it was cruel and hurtful. She was so angry that she decided to sue Marjorie for libel. Zelma wanted to prove to a judge and jury that Marjorie had lied about her in *Cross Creek.*

The trial began on Monday, May 20, 1946. It was still spring, but Florida's summer heat had already started. The hot, sticky courtroom was crowded with onlookers eager to get a chance to see the famous author. People sat mopping their brows and fanning their faces, while beads of perspiration trickled down their backs.

At the time, it was against the law in Florida for women to serve on juries, so the jury consisted of six young men, all from Florida. Marjorie's lawyers brought in many witnesses, some of whom were friends and neighbors of both Marjorie and Zelma. Some of them had also been described by Marjorie in *Cross Creek.* They could have sided with Zelma, but they didn't.

Marjorie had once been an outsider at Cross Creek, but in her years there, she had proven that she was a true friend. The people who spoke in court told the jury that they didn't believe Marjorie meant any harm with her book. They believed that she had simply described the people and places of Cross Creek as she saw them.

The trial lasted for seven days. When it was over, the jury took only twenty-eight minutes to reach its decision. They found Marjorie not guilty. She was thrilled and relieved. But Zelma was determined that the matter would not rest. She and her lawyer took the case to the Florida Supreme Court for another trial. There would be another year of fighting in court unless Marjorie agreed that she had done something wrong by writing about Zelma.

The court case was wearing Marjorie down, but she was too stubborn to give in to Zelma's point of view. Marjorie believed that she was fighting for the rights of all writers and artists, not just for herself. Marjorie's lawyer, Phil May, wrote to the Florida Supreme Court in support of Marjorie. He said that the case would make history. He and Marjorie hoped it would show that authors must be free to take their experiences and weave them into their stories. Unfortunately, the Court did not agree with Marjorie and her lawyer. They reversed the jury's decision and found Marjorie guilty of "invasion of privacy." She was only fined one dollar, but she had still lost the case.

It had been five years since *Cross Creek* was published and Zelma first decided to sue Marjorie. The trial had been very hard on Marjorie, both physically and financially. She was exhausted when it was all over. And she was deeply hurt that someone from the Creek had turned against her. But she had done her best to defend the rights of authors, and she had been encouraged by other writers to do so. To her, the case had been a fight for "the right of anyone to write of his or her own life."

Afterword

Marjorie had lost her case in court, but she did not lose her many fans. Children and adults continued to read her books and write letters to her. Popular movies were made from several of her books, including *The Yearling*. And Marjorie was asked to give lectures all over the country.

Marjorie and Norton were happy through the remaining years of their marriage. She traveled a great deal, and they both respected each other's independence. Norton stayed in Florida to manage the Castle Warden, but Marjorie often spent time at a house she owned in New York State to work on her writing. The books she published in her later years were successful, but nothing ever came close to the success she had enjoyed with *The Yearling.*

In mid-December 1953, Marjorie was in the middle of working on a new book. She was at her Crescent Beach cottage with Norton when she began to feel ill. On December 18, a blood vessel in her brain burst. Norton rushed her to the hospital, where she died. She was fifty-seven years old.

After she died, her books and her life continued to interest readers. A movie called *Cross Creek,* based on the book about her years in Florida, was made in 1983. Marjorie was remembered as someone who didn't often take no for an answer. She never gave up on her dream of becoming a great success as a writer. And she didn't let anyone stand in her way. She lived alone for a long time in a place that some people considered uncivilized. She did many things that were considered unladylike and improper during her time. But she presented herself with a directness and simplicity that usually won over her critics. Marjorie was a complex person who could be difficult at times. But she was a woman who stood by her convictions.

Marjorie is buried at Antioch Cemetery, only a few miles away from her farm at Cross Creek. She is surrounded by the trees and wildlife that she loved.

Many of her friends and neighbors, including Zelma Cason, are laid to rest nearby. Marjorie's gravestone is inscribed with the words: "Through her writing she endeared herself to the people of the world."

Marjorie's home at Cross Creek has been protected as a state historic site. It is a glimpse into the past and into this unique woman's life. The farm and orange grove are still operating and productive. Marjorie's car remains parked next to the farmhouse, and her typewriter still sits on a table on the porch. Cross Creek has become a tribute to both the beauty of the Florida landscape and the popularity of one of Florida's best-known writers.

Books by Marjorie Kinnan Rawlings

1933 *South Moon Under*

1935 *Golden Apples*

1938 *The Yearling*

1940 *When the Whippoorwill*

1942 *Cross Creek*

1942 *Cross Creek Cookery*

1953 *The Sojourner*

1955 *The Secret River* (posthumously)

Bibliography

Acton, Patricia Nassif. *Invasion of Privacy.* Gainesville, FL: University of Florida Press, 1988.

Bellman, Samuel I. *Marjorie Kinnan Rawlings.* Boston: Twayne Publishers, 1974.

Bigelow, Gordon E. *Frontier Eden.* Gainesville, FL: University of Florida Press, 1966.

Bigelow, Gordon E., and Laura V. Monti, eds. *Selected Letters of Marjorie Kinnan Rawlings.* Gainesville, FL: University Press of Florida, 1983.

Parker, Idella. *Idella, Marjorie Rawlings' "Perfect Maid."* Gainesville, FL: University Press of Florida, 1992.

Perkins, Maxwell E. *Max & Marjorie: The Correspondence between Maxwell E. Perkins & Marjorie Kinnan Rawlings.* Gainesville, FL: University Press of Florida, 1999.

Rawlings, Marjorie Kinnan. *Cross Creek.* New York: Charles Scribner's Sons, 1942.

Rawlings, Marjorie Kinnan. *Songs of a Housewife.* Gainesville, FL: University Press of Florida, 1997.

Rawlings, Marjorie Kinnan. *The Yearling.* New York: Charles Scribner's Sons, 1939.

Silverthorne, Elizabeth. *Marjorie Kinnan Rawlings, Sojourner at Cross Creek.* Woodstock, NY: The Overlook Press, 1988.

Index

About the Authors

Mother-daughter writing team **Judy Cook** and **Laura Lee Smith** can easily relate to Marjorie Kinnan Rawlings's fascination with Florida's landscape and its people. They too fell in love with their adopted state.

Originally from New Jersey, the Cooks moved to south Florida when Laura was eleven years old. Judy juggled a career as a legal assistant with a busy family life for many years. After her three children grew up, she began to write and publish articles. Judy lives in Jacksonville, Florida.

Laura earned a B.A. in literature and an M.A. in English from the University of North Florida. A long-time freelance writer, Laura has written articles for a number of regional and national publications. She lives in Atlantic Beach, Florida, with her husband, Chris, and their children, Iain and Gemma.

About the Illustrator

As a child growing up in Morris County, New Jersey, **Laurie Harden** was surrounded by an artistic family. She later studied painting at the Kansas City Art Institute and then completed her B.F.A. at the Rhoda Island School of Design, where she studied illustration and printmaking. Laurie has illustrated several books for children and young adults. She is also an award-winning artist whose work is known both nationally and internationally. Laurie lives in Morris County with her husband and two sons.